Legends of India's Temples

Manoj Das

 is an imprint of

BUSINESS PUBLICATIONS INC

ISBN 81-7693-024-5
© Manoj Das 1999
Cover design Akshay Dange

Published by

NĒVĒ

229/A Krantiveer Rajguru Marg
Girgaon, Mumbai 400 004
Tel : 3808817/19 Fax : 3872625
E-mail : bpipl@vsnl.com

CONTENTS

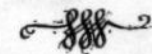

*If the measurement of the temple
is in every way perfect,
There will be perfection
in the universe as well.*

MAYAMATA

The Sun Temple ~ Konarak

THE GRAND SHRINE OF THE SUN-GOD

The Black Pagoda of Konarak

It was a clear morning, hundreds of years ago. A smart lad was taking leave of his mother on the outskirts of a small village. The mother, tears rolling down her cheeks, looked on till her son disappeared behind a mound of sand where the road took a turn.

The boy walked on and on. Hours later, his own village, with the peak of the familiar temple and the spires of tall trees, became only a dark line on the horizon. He had never come away that far alone and he had yet to go a long distance.

He left behind him many a village. He spent the night in a village choultry and resumed his journey in the morning.

At last, on the other side of a green wood, he saw the summit of a huge monument. It looked bright in the sun. The boy's face beamed with delight. As he advanced, he could see hundreds of men working on the building, and from that distance they looked as small as ants. They were building a temple that was designed to surpass all the monuments of the country in size and grandeur. The boy's mission was to meet one of the builders.

It did not take him long to find the man he sought, for he was the leader of the builders, the chief architect of the unique monument.

The boy's voice was choked as he stood face-to-face with the celebrated architect. He was so moved that it was hard for him to control his tears. But he somehow managed to give the architect a souvenir which his mother had sent with him.

What followed, was a moment of great ecstasy for both the architect and the boy. Everyone present looked on with surprise, as their leader hugged and kissed the lad.

In no time, everybody learnt who the boy was. They greeted their little guest, Dharmapada, the only child of the chief architect, Bishu Maharana. Dharmapada was an infant when Maharana left his house. Twelve years had

passed. There had been no meeting between father and son. The young Dharmapada had at last come to surprise his father.

Dharmapada joyfully surveyed the beautiful site on which the great temple had been built. Surging waves of the sea continuously played around the compound wall. When the tide was in, the temple was encircled by the sea. To the west of the temple flowed the murmuring Chanrabhaga, a holy river.

It was a sacred place and had been the seat of the Sun God from time immemorial. Sages and mystics knew about the place even during the days of Lord Krishna. When Shambo, the son of Lord Krishna, suffered from an incurable disease, he was advised to come here and to worship the Sun God. He did so and was cured. That had made the place very famous. The great temple was to be dedicated to the Sun God.

The mighty, visionary king of Kalinga, Narasimha Dev, had summoned 1200 skilled architects, sculptors and craftsmen from all over his kingdom to build this temple. He had asked his able minister, Shibei Samantroy, to supervise the work. In front of the young Dharmapada

stood the splendid achievement of his father and his gifted assistants. Only the crown of the temple remained to be set.

Dharmapada had learnt to read from a very young age. He would studiously go through the volumes of palm-leaves left at home by his father. They contained information about the art and science of building monuments. Dharmapada had learnt many theories and he was now thrilled to see a huge temple, in which many difficult theories had been put into practice.

While he marvelled at the sight, he felt that there was a sense of gloom in the atmosphere. The architects who should have been happy, as twelve years of their strenuous labour was now about to be completed, looked pensive. He wanted to know the reason for their sadness from his father.

Bishu Maharana, at first reluctant to utter a word, could not check himself for long. He almost broke down as he said, "My son, a great crisis has befallen us. We are faced with a problem in adjusting the crown of the temple. For several days we have been trying to solve it, but without success. It is sufficient to drive us crazy. We

are ashamed to call ourselves the descendants of the great builders of yore.

"Then, to add to our agony, this morning the king told us that if we cannot complete the work before the sun rises again, tomorrow will be our doomsday."

Evening was setting in. The temple still wore the soothing rays of the hidden sun. Soon a full moon emerged from the sea and all was enchanting beneath it.

When the architects gathered inside a large hall to discuss the crisis, Dharmapada, unnoticed by them, ascended the temple. He surveyed the position of the crown and reflected deeply on the problem. Suddenly, the solution flashed in his vision! Theories were still fresh in his mind. His father and the others had perhaps grown tired, working so hard for years, and the solution had kept evading their minds.

Dharmapada came down and entered the conference hall. He humbly put forth his idea before his elders. They immediately knew, that what he said was the right solution. Delighted and excited, some of them went up the temple and set the crown in its proper position, following Dharmapada's directions.

Dharmapada was a hero now. As he came, everybody greeted him joyfully and praised him.

But in every age, there are people who are jealous of the achievements of others. Dharmapada soon overhead some people talking among themselves :"What will the king say when he hears that a boy has done what 1200 experts failed to do? Here is Dharmapada to take our reputation away!"

Dharmapada was shocked. He retired to a lonely spot and thought, "I do not wish to deprive these noble workers of their glory." When all were asleep and the moon shone in its full glory, Dharmapada again climbed to the top of the temple – now complete with the crown. The sea had swelled with the tide and gold-fringed waves danced madly around the temple. Dharmapada looked at the sleeping men below and prayed that their reputation would remain ever-shining. He then jumped from a height of 69 metres into the sea below.

In the morning, the king was happy to see the crown set. He congratulated the craftsmen. Bishu Maharana perhaps kept quiet, his anguish buried deep in his heart.

Thus goes the legend of Dharmapada. His great, but sad role in completing the construction of Konarak, soon came to light and has never been forgotten.

Hundreds of years have passed. On a desolate coastal spot in Orissa, the remains of Konarak, often called the Black Pagoda, is counted among the wonders of the world. The image of the Sun God has disappeared. Even the main temple has been completely destroyed. Only the *Mukhasala,* or the fore-temple, survives with its carvings of indescribable beauty. Stones have never responded so well to the demands of the craftsmen's instruments.

The temple was designed to look like a chariot, with 24 magnificent wheels and seven horses. Authorities on sculpture say that these images of horses are among the finest in the world.

The temple has inspired deep admiration through the ages. Abdul Fazl, the famous minister of Akbar, wrote in his *Ain-i-Akbari,* "Near Jaganath (Puri) is a temple dedicated to the Sun. Twelve years' revenue of the country was spent on it. Experts, difficult to please, are struck with amazement on seeing it. The height of its walls is a hundred and fifty hands and their thickness, nineteen. It has three doorways. On the eastern one are figures of two elephants nicely carved, each catching hold of a man on its trunk; on the western door figures of two horsemen have been set up with all equipment and splendour; and on the northern side there is a likeness of two lions each

making prey of an elephant and standing rampant on it. In front is an octagonal pillar of black stone, fifty yards in height. On ascending the nine flights of steps one sees a spacious enclosure and a large niche, built in stone in which has been carved the Sun with other planets….They say seven hundred and odd years ago Raja Narasimha Dev finished this grand building…."

Abdul Fazl wrote his account in the latter half of the 16th century. If we are to accept the time he ascribes to Narasimha Dev, then we have to believe that Konarak was completed in the ninth century. But historians think otherwise. Most of them believe that the temple was constructed in the 13th century.

The main temple of Konarak was the highest in India. There is a legend which says that the crown of the temple contained a gigantic magnet which pulled ships ashore. Some harassed foreign merchants therefore, removed it and consequently the whole temple collapsed.

Others say that it was Kalapahar, the scourge of Hindu monuments, who destroyed the temple. There are others who think that an earthquake must have caused the destruction.

Modern engineers and architects wonder how the gigantic stones – some of them weighing 2000 tons – were brought from distant hills and lifted and fixed at a height of 200 feet ! In the first decade of our century, when it was necessary to remove some of the scattered panels of the ruined temple to another place, gunpowder had to be used to break them into smaller pieces! A historian satirically observed, "When the stones were put up in the temple, they were light. Being soaked in rain for seven hundred years, they must have grown heavy!"

The Goddess of Eternal Hope

The Temple of Kanya Kumari

There is a spot from which one can at once see the waters of three seas. That is Kanya Kumari or Cape Comorin – the 'Lands' End' of India. There you can see the sun rise over the Bay of Bengal and set over the Arabian Sea. If you keep the Bay of Bengal to your left and the Arabian Sea to your right, the expanse of water in front of you is the Indian Ocean.

If you stoop down and pick up a handful of small pebbles you will notice that they are of varied colours. And if any old man of the locality sees you appreciating the pebbles, he might stop to tell you why they are so.

They are sweetened, fragrant, coloured rice, turned into small pebbles. Then, during the course of the conversation, he may tell you one of the saddest legends you have ever heard.

In the days of yore, the land was threatened by a demon-king, Vanasura. Even the gods were terrorised. The Divine Mother, with the purpose of getting rid of the demon, descended upon the earth as the daughter of a monarch who lived at Land's End.

She grew up to be a beautiful princess. Her father now thought of her marriage and looked around for a suitable bridegroom. The goddess, who had momentarily forgotten about her divine self, suddenly woke up to the fact that there was no question of her marrying a mortal. If marry she must, she must wed Shiva, her eternal consort.

The princess meditated on Shiva. On Mount Kailas, the abode of the great god, Shiva woke up from his deep trance and knew that it was time for him to go down to the far south and marry the princess. The auspicious hour for the marriage was fixed. The ritual was to be performed at midnight.

Shiva descended from his citadel of snow, sufficiently in advance of the time, and started walking towards Land's End. But the proposed marriage made the

gods and the sages pensive. The goddess had taken birth as a princess to kill Vanasura. She could do this only while she was still a maiden. If she married Shiva and went away to Kailas, the very purpose of her incarnation would be defeated.

Narada, the clever sage, was requested to do something about it. He assumed the form of a cock, and hiding under a bush at Land's End, he crowed loudly. The absent-minded Shiva was shocked to hear the cock. He felt sure that the auspicious hour had passed and that it was already dawn. He sat down remorsefully. And for him, sitting down, only meant entering a deep trance.

Thus Shiva never reached the bride's home. He remains in Suchindrum temple,

Soon Vanasura, who had heard about the charming princess, appeared on the scene a few miles away from Kanya Kumari, towards the interior of the land. He demanded to marry her. When his demand was turned down, he tried to take her away forcibly. The princess took hold of a sword and, after a brief combat, put an end to the audacious demon.

The princess, in her bridal attire waited for a long time for Shiva. The rice that had been cooked for the wedding feast turned, in course of time, into tiny pebbles. That is why the pebbles are so colourful at Kanya Kumari.

The goddess still stands inside the last monument on the Indian land in the farthest south. The image of the deity is extremely beautiful. She looks eastward, the horizon of the rising sun, and awaits the arrival of Shiva. Thus she symbolises eternal hope. She is also the presiding deity of the sacred Indian border. She killed the demon and herself emerged unscathed, showing that eternal India was inviolable.

The small hills, with bushes and woods, and the miles and miles of coconut trees through which one passes on one's way to Kanya Kumari, remain ever green in her memory. The temple of Kanya Kumari is not an imposing building, but it has been considered most sacred for many centuries. The deity was once worshipped by the famous Pandya kings who ruled the Tamil region for hundreds of years. The temple, which we see today, appears to have been built by them over an old one, in the 12th or the 13th century.

In the month of October, the Navaratri festival takes place. It commemorates Kanya Kumari's victory over Vanasura. The battle between the goddess, the incarnation of purity and truth, and Vanasura, the personification of lust and pride, is enacted in an interesting manner. This is perhaps to remind man that the conflict is not yet over.

THE SHRINE BUILT
BY NATURE

The Abode of Amarnath

"To him the heavens had opened. He had touched the feet of Shiva. He had to hold himself tight, he said afterwards, lest he should swoon away … 'I have enjoyed it so much!' he said half an hour afterwards. 'I never enjoyed any religious place so much !' He always said, that the grace of Amarnath had been granted to him there, not to die till he himself should give consent. And to me he said, 'You do not understand. But you have made the pilgrimage and it will go on working. Causes must bring their effects. You will understand better afterwards. The effects will come."

Do you know who was about to swoon away inside the cave-temple of Amarnath? It was Swami Vivekananda. The above record is left by Sister Nivedita.

Vivekananda felt the living presence of Lord Shiva in Amarnath and he was also granted a boon. Others might not have had as great a spiritual experience as Vivekananda, but such is the lure of Amarnath that year after year, thousands of people pay homage there, despite the difficulties they encounter on the way.

Amarnath is situated in Kashmir, in the hinterland of rocks and snow, at a height of about 4000 metres. For a greater part of the year, the region remains shrouded in snow and mystery. From September to June, nature denies all access to human beings. The mouth of the cave opens only in August, which happens to be the rainy season in the region. But pilgrims brave the rain and trek uphill from Pahalgam. The journey takes them about a week.

"Umbrellas are held up not so much to shelter their owners as to prevent the fires being extinguished and the food being spoilt. Men in saffron-coloured robes, drenched to the skin, move about or huddle together in groups," describes a pilgrim.

Along the route taken by the pilgrims, flows the river Dudh Ganga, like a never-ending line of white birds flying and flapping their wings. Its water is almost milk-white. As one reaches Panjtarini, one is charmed by the sight of five rivers flowing side by side. Mount Kailas and Mount Vairo stand like sentinels over the serene silence of the region, their towering presence adding to its majesty.

Finally, one stands inside the eight-metre-high cave temple, deeply moved by the peace that prevails there. Many feel the presence of a divinity in the atmosphere.

It is not a man-made shrine. It is a cave, a dwelling on earth for the Divine, made by Nature. No man-made idol is to be seen either. Icicles slowly grow to form the symbol of Shiva. The symbol increases in size with the waxing of the moon and decreases with the waning. Pilgrims consider this phenomenon a miracle.

It is said that a shephered boy once entered this desolate area in search of his lost lamb and rediscovered the cave that lay forgotten for a long time. He carried the news to the king of Kashmir, who hurried to have a look at the place himself, and soon it became known to the people.

It must have been a long, long time ago. We know from the *Rajatarangini,* which is a record of events in Sanskrit verse written in the 12th century, that pilgrims went to Amarnath long before the book was written.

But why is Amarnath a sacred place? 'Amarnath' literally means 'Lord of Immortality'. Legend says that once Parvati asked Shiva, "You are the God of gods. Can you not find a garland made of anything better then skulls? "

"These skulls are very precious to me, since they happen to be yours! You have taken birth and have been my wife many times. Every time you die, your skull is collected and added to this garland," answered Shiva.

Parvati was amazed. "Why do I die while you remain immortal ?" she asked.

"That is because I know the mysteries that make one immortal," replied Shiva.

"You must disclose those mysteries to me," said Parvati, and she insisted on knowing them.

Shiva looked for a place where no living creature could be found, for he did not want his narration to be heard by anyone. He finally selected a cave and sat inside it with Parvati by his side. He asked his spirit-servants to drive away all the living creatures from that area. The spirits

carried out the order faithfully and with as much alacrity as they could.

Shiva then started narrating the mysteries of immortality to Parvati. From time to time Parvati said, "Hm." That was the indication that she listened to him with great attention. Shiva went on for many hours. When he finished, he realized that Parvati had fallen asleep while he had been talking. Who then could have kept repeating "Hm"?

Shiva suddenly saw a tiny *shuka*, a parrot, come out from under the rock on which he sat and fly away in the twinkle of an eye. Shiva's able servants had driven away all creatures from the entire area, but it had not occurred to them to look under the seat of their master. Inside lay an egg. The chick had come out of its shell while Shiva spoke. It listened to the narration and responded when Parvati fell asleep.

Now, as the bird flew away, Shiva pursued it. Far away was the hut of Vyasa, the great sage. In the courtyard of the hut, his wife was sitting and combing her hair. As she pulled the comb through her hair, her mouth was open for a moment. The little parrot flew into her mouth. Shiva soon reached there, but could do nothing.

In the womb of Vyasa's wife, the bird was transformed into a human child. He remained in her womb for 12 years. Finally he came out and was acknowledged as a great seer. He was called Shukadeva.

The cave in which Shiva revealed the secret of immortality is the cave-temple of Amarnath, one of the holiest of places. With the right attitude, one can have a great spiritual experience there.

The Meenakshi Temple ~ Madurai

The Princess Who was The Divine Mother

Meenakshi's Temple At Madurai

Indra, the King of Heaven, was once challenged by a demon hero, Britta. On the banks of the Manasarovara in the Himalayas, a fierce battle was fought between the two and it continued for 100 years. Indra of course, finally killed the demon, but he did that more through a trick than through his strength.

Though Britta was a demon, he had performed years of penance through which he had gained the virtues of a Brahmin. To kill a Brahmin was a great sin. Awful consequences were bound to follow.

Indra wandered on earth repenting and praying for purification. One day, as he was passing through a dense forest near the ancient kingdom of Kalyanpur, he suddenly felt a certain peace in his heart.

"This forest seems to be a blessed place!" Indra told himself and surveyed it carefully. Soon he came across a piece of stone which appeared to be the symbol of Lord Shiva. Indra camped there and spent a long time worshipping the symbol. By Shiva's grace, his period of agony was over and he returned to heaven.

The King of Kalyanpur was a pious man. He realised that the forest was blessed with Shiva's presence. He built his capital there. But he could not decide what the name of the new city should be.

One night, the king dreamt that Shiva was sprinkling sweet nectar over the city. The king took the hint and named his new capital Madhurapura, the Sweet City. In course of time Madhurapura came to be called Madurai.

Madurai is perhaps the oldest city in South India. It is famous all over the world for its grand temple of Goddess Meenakshi, which stands in the centre of the city.

About three thousand years ago, the king of Vijayanagar performed a sacrifice in the hope of gaining a

son. But his wife gave birth to a daughter. She was named Meenakshi – 'Meena' meaning fish, and 'Akshi' meaning eye. In ancient India the fish was an ideal simile for well-shaped eyes.

Meenakshi succeeded her father to the throne. She was beautiful, brave and noble. As her fame spread far and wide, the rulers of nearby kingdoms became jealous of her. On some silly excuse they marched into her realm together, sure of defeating her and sharing her kingdom among themselves.

Meenakshi stormed into the invading armies. As she rode through them, her sword sizzled and flashed like lightning, striking them down by the dozen. Soon all of them fell at her feet, either dead or in submission.

Meenakshi galloped forth to see if there were more enemies hiding inside the forest. Suddenly a stranger emerged before her. She raised her sword, taking the stranger to be an enemy-king. But on looking at him, she blushed. He was none other than Shiva. Meenakshi was really Parvati.

So they met on the earth and were married. The marriage was a great occasion of joy for both men and gods.

A slightly embarrassing situation arose when one of the chief attendants of Shiva, Gondodara, chose to express his joy in a novel way. He went on eating. Time and again his plates were filled, but were soon empty. Day and night he sat eating, till the food minister of the bride's palace was on the verge of a nervous breakdown. He at last reported the matter to Meenakshi. The smiling Meenakshi, came out with a dish of sweets and gave them to Gondodara. He finished them greatfully and got up, thoroughly satisfied.

Gondodara then wanted to drink water. If the quantity of food he had devoured was any indication of the quantity of water he might wish to drink, then there was no use trying to satisfy him with the water that could be drawn from the well in the palace. Meenakshi said to him, "Bhaigai!" which meant, "Put your hand down!" Gondodara obeyed her. At once there sprang up a river under his hand. He drank to his heart's content. The river known as Vaigai, flows on to this day.

The temple complex of Meenakshi, which includes the shrine of Shiva, known as Sun-dareswara, strikes one as magnificent. Monuments belonging to the outer parts

of the old temple were destroyed by Malik Kafur who invaded Madurai in the early 14th century. Luckily, he did not get a chance to destroy the shrines of Meenakshi and Sundareswara because a serious quarrel broke out among his soldiers and he had to retreat in haste.

Viswanath Naik, who ruled Madurai in the 16th century, began rebuilding the temple. Generations of rulers contributed to make the complex as grand and vast as we see it today.

There are ten majestic *gopurams* (gateways) around the temple. One is immediately struck by the grandeur of the four outer *gopurams*. They look alike, but the motifs of the charming carvings on them are all different. The southern pillar is 46 metres high – the highest of all. Near this are the five musical pillars. Each pillar has 22 bars carved out of a single block of granite. When tapped they produce melodious musical sounds.

The other interesting feature of the temple is a hall with 1000 pillars full of lovely sculptures. This was built in the 16th century.

There is the Golden Lotus Tank, said to be the pool in which Indra bathed. For a long time, a literary academy used to hold its sessions near the tank. It was

believed that if a new manuscript, when thrown into the tank, floated instead of sinking, it had true value.

The goddess Meenakshi has a brother nearby. He is Sri Sundarajaswami, the deity of Alagar temple. About 18 kilometres to the north-east of Madurai, the temple is situated at the bottom of a nine-kilometre-high hill with a cool spring at its top. The deity of Alagar comes once in a year to the city of his sister. There are several *mandapams* on the route where the deity rests on his way to and from Madurai.

WHERE VISHNU SAT
IN SOLITUDE

The Temple of Tirupati

The Peak of Mount Sheshachalam in the Eastern Ghat range was so tranquil and enchanting a place, that the sage Narada spoke highly of it to Vishnu.

Vishnu felt tempted to pay a visit to the place, but there was no occasion for him to do so.

Some time later Vishnu had a dispute with his wife, Lakshmi. Vishnu left home and came down to earth. He had to be away, not only from his wife, but also from all the gods, goddesses and human beings. He remembered Sheshachalam and proceeded there.

Vishnu was charmed with the range of seven blue peaks adorned by green woods. He sat down to meditate.

Time passed – God knows how long! An ant-hill grew around the meditating Vishnu and covered him completely.

It was the curiosity of a shepherd that finally revealed Vishnu's secret seat. The shepherd had a cow which often disappeared into the forest. One day the shepherd followed the cow stealthily. The cow entered the forest, climbed a mountain and stood over the ant-hill. Then, most unusually, milk began flowing from her on to the ant-hill.

The shepherd was filled with awe and amazement. He could not muster the courage to go near the ant-hill, but he rushed to the city and narrated his experience to the king.

The king reached the area and soon discovered an image of Vishnu under the ant-hill. He erected a beautiful shrine on the mountain. The deity came to be known as Tirupati Balaji.

Lakshmi could not endure her separation from Vishnu for long. She found out where Vishnu was. She took birth as a princess and took the name of Padmavati.

Balaji often assumed a human form to roam in the forest. One day, while wandering in the forest, he saw the charming Padmavati and recognised her instantly. The celestial couple re-enacted their marriage on earth.

The temple to Balaji as we see it today, was most probably built by King Thondaman of the Chola dynasty. Thondaman ruled over a vast kingdom in the first century. The main temple is a fine example of South Indian architecture and the *Vimana* over the sanctum, is covered with gold.

The temple, in Andhra Pradesh, attracts lakhs of devotees and tourists every year, many of whom come with handsome offerings. It is one of the richest institutions in India. Much of the temple's wealth is spent in supporting various social, cultural and educational institutions.

The deity was well-known long before the present temple was built. It is believed that Rama, Sita and Lakshmana visited the deity and spent some time there. The spot where they are said to have rested is known as Swamitirtha.

Hundreds of years later the Pandavas too, came there and spent a year on one of the peaks, which is known to this day as the Pandava Shringha.

At a height of four-and-a-half kilometres, the seat of Tirupati, surrounded by waterfalls, is deservedly a chosen place of God.

Where an Incarnation Worshipped Shiva

The Temple of Rameswaram

Sita was stolen by Ravana, the demon king of Lanka, and Rama prepared to invade Lanka in order to rescue her. Accompanied by wise advisers and devoted followers, he arrived at the southern point of the Indian land. But how were they to cross the sea to reach Lanka? Rama decided to build a bridge with rocks and stones, over which his soldiers could march on to the island.

Another problem soon surfaced. Though Rama's army worked hard during the day at building the bridge, at night Ravana's demons destroyed their work. This happened time and again. Then one of the wise ministers of Rama, Jambavan, said, "Let us build a temple for Shiva

on the bridge. Ravana, who is a devotee of Shiva, would never destroy the bridge with his Lord's temple on it."

So a temple to Shiva was built, and indeed, the bridge was no longer destroyed by Ravana.

This is one of the two popular legends behind the temple of Rameswaram.

According to the other legend, the temple was built by Rama not before his invasion of Lanka, but after it.

The days of the battle were full of tension and strain. By the time victory came to him, Rama was very tired. In the flying chariot, Pushpak, he returned to India with Sita by his side. They alighted on the first bit of Indian land they saw. Standing on the seashore, they were overwhelmed with a sense of gratitude and wished to worship Shiva.

But a symbol of Shiva was necessary for worship. Hanuman rushed to Varanasi to fetch the famous deity, Viswanath. But Viswanath declined to come.

Hanuman then went to the Himalayas to get a stone that could be installed as the symbol of Shiva.

It look a long time for him to find the right kind of stone. At last, when he hurried back with the precious object to the seashore, he saw that his master had already begun to worship a symbol which Sita had moulded out of earth.

Hanuman felt depressed. Rama comforted him with loving words and assured him that the stone he had brought would not only be worshipped, but would also be worshipped first.

So it happens to this day; before a devotee can worship Rameswaram, the deity founded by Rama, he has to worship Visweswara, the deity brought by Hanuman. Both, of course, are manifestations of Shiva.

The temple of Rameswaram is situated on a small island off the south-eastern coast of India. The island is said to resemble the shape of *Pancha-janya,* the conch of Lord Krishna.

The temple we see today was built by King Udayana of the Setupati dynasty, in the fifteenth century. Later, several rulers added buildings, walls and *gopurams* to the main shrine.

The 1200-metre-long corridor, with 1000 magnificent pillars, is a unique feature of the Rameswaram temple.

The temple is also viewed as a reminder of the bond that exists between India and Sri Lanka since the king of Sri Lanka, Pararaj Shekhar, contributed generously to its construction.

Besides, Rameswaram is one of the four celebrated Hindu *Dhams* – holiest of holy places.

Home of the Lord of the Universe ~ Puri

The Lord
Of the Universe

The Temple of Jagannath at Puri

In days of yore, Indradyumna ruled over a vast territory. He had conquered many lands and had earned great fame, but he always felt the urge to do something different, something more lofty.

At last he decided to build a large temple. He sat down with his architects and made a plan for the building. But unless there was a genuine, living deity to dwell in the temple, what was the use of building it?

One night he had a remarkable dream. He saw a small hill in the interior of an unknown forest. There was

a cave in the hill and in the cave dwelt a beautiful deity, who represented the Lord of the Universe, or Jagannath.

Indradyumna did not know where the hill was, but he was most anxious to find out. So he sent four Brahmins to trace the hill and the deity.

Months passed. One of the wandering Brahmins, a young man named Vidyapati, reached a wooded land inhabited by the Sabaras, an ancient tribe. He arrived at the house of their chief, Viswavasu, seeking shelter. Viswavasu was very pleased to play host to Vidyapati, who was a wise scholar and a charming personality.

Vidyapati intutively felt a spiritual atmosphere in that part of the forest. He decided to live there for some time.

Viswavasu had a beautiful daughter called Lolita. It so happened that Vidyapati earned not only the affection of the chief, but also the love of Lolita. Soon he married her and continued to live there.

During the course of his stay, Vidyapati observed that Viswavasu went out into the forest everyday before dawn and came back after sunrise. Even a storm would not prevent him from doing so.

"Where does your father go early in the morning?" Vidyapati asked Lolita one day.

"O my husband, though I am not supposed to reveal this to anyone, how can I hide anything from you? My father goes out to worship Nilamadhav, inside the cave in Nilachala," she replied.

Vidyapati was thrilled to hear this. At once he had a feeling that what he sought was here! "Where is Nilachala? Won't you take me there?" he pleaded with Lolita. Soon Viswavasu same to know of his son-in-law's eagerness to see Nilamadhav. He reluctantly agreed to take Vidyapati there, but only on the condition that the latter's eyes were covered.

While Vidyapati was led to Nilachala blindfolded, he scattered mustard seeds on the way, un-noticed by Viswavasu. After a few days, following a shower of rain, leaves sprouted from the mustard seeds and it was not difficult for Vidyapati to find the way to the cave.

One day Vidyapati took leave of Lolita and Viswavasu to pay a visit to his home. On his way, he stole the idol from the cave and hurried to the court of King Indradyumna. Viswavasu was not to know of his loss until the next morning.

Indradyumna was very happy when he saw the image of Nilamadhav. But his joy did not last long. When

the Sabara chief saw that his deity had been stolen, he was about to end his life in grief. Knowing his devotee's love for him, the deity mysteriously disappeared from the palace of Indrayumna.

Expecting to find the idol in the cave of Nilochala, Indrayumna hurried there. But the cave was about to torture him when he heard a voice telling him to first build a temple in which to house the deity. Only then would the deity come to him.

The king now devoted all his energy, imagination and wealth to build a majestic temple.

Many years later, when the temple was complete, the king was told in a dream to go to the seashore and collect a floating log. The image of Jagannath would be carved out of it and in this new form, would dwell Nilamadhav.

The king rushed to the seashore and saw a log floating nearby. But in spite of all his efforts, he could not bring it ashore. The king in utter despair, decided to kill himself. At night, however, he was directed in a vision to seek the help of Viswavasu.

The king sent a messenger to Viswavasu and requested him to come there. As soon as Viswavasu

touched the wood, it proved light. Thus did the deity prove his love for both his devotees – the king and Viswavasu.

However, there soon arose a fresh problem. No craftsman could be found who would undertake to carve the image of Jagannath out of the wood. Just when the king had started to despair again, an old man appeared before him and offered to do the job. He was a very old man, but there was something extraordinary about him which impressed the king. The stranger however, laid one condition: nobody should open the doors of his room until 21 days were over. That was the time he needed to finish the work.

The old man then started his work inside a closed room. Every day, the queen pressed her ear against the door of the room and heard sounds made by the mysterious craftsman. But after a fortnight, she stopped hearing anything. This went on for a few days. One day she lost all patience. She thought that the old man was dead!

She pushed the doors open suddenly. The old man cast a look at her and disappeared, leaving the three images of Jagannath, his brother Balarama, and their sister Subhadra, incomplete, as they are seen to this day.

The old man was none other than the godly architect and sculptor, Viswakarma.

The king, however, assumed that it was ordained that such should be the forms of the deities. Viswavasu too, was delighted to see them. His old deity was put inside the form of Jagannath.

Till today the descendants of Viswavasu, the Sabara chief, are among the priests of the temple of Lord Jagannath at Puri.

Another legend says that after the temple was constructed, it lay forgotten, buried under sand for hundreds of years. One day, while King Galamadhav was galloping across a sandy stretch of land, his horse faltered as its hoof struck something hard. The king got down and examined the object. It seemed to be the top of a temple. At the king's command the sand was removed and the wonderful monument, 58 metres in height, was discovered.

According to historians the temple of Jagannath was built in the 12th century by the Ganga kings of Kalinga. It required great vision, great dedication and a great amount of wealth. All these were present with the Ganga kings – particularly Choda Ganga Dev, the greatest of them all.

Magnificent is the temple for its varied sculptures as delicate as the traditional filigree work of Orissa.

About 200,000 people flock to Puri every year in the month of June to witness or participate in the famous Car Festival of the deities. Jagannath, Balarama, and Subhadra are taken on three huge wooden chariots with 16 wheels each, to another shrine about two kilometres away from the main temple. The festival commemorates Krishna's journey from Gokula to Mathura. It is said that the relics of Krishna are contained in the image of Jagannath. Perhaps what Viswavasu treasured and worshipped as Nilamadhav are the relics of Krishna.

Some people believe that Buddha's tooth is also there. Chaitanya dev, the great prophet of Vaishnavism, is said to have disappeared while concentrating on the image inside the temple. Thus, Jagannath is associated with many traditions.

No wonder that of all the Hindu seats of pilgrimage, Puri draws the largest number of pilgrims.

The Legendary Kingdom of Krishna ~ Dwaraka

Where Krishna ruled
as a King

The Temple of Dwaraka

Dwaraka or Dwaravati, was the city where Krishna lived as king. Naturally, it is one of the four sacred *Dhams* of India. The legendary city of Dwaraka was not made by men. After Krishna chose the site it was Viswakarma, heaven's architect, who planned and built the city. Shiva and Kuvera, from Kailas and Patal respectively, sent their spirit-servants to execute the plans drawn by Viswakarma. When the construction of the city was complete, it looked like a chunk of paradise!

Before the Kurukshetra war began, both the Pandavas and the Kauravas were eager to avail of Krishna's support for themselves.

Duryodhana came to Dwaraka to meet Krishna on behalf of the Kauravas. At that time Krishna was asleep in his palace. Duryodhana sat on a luxurious seat close to Krishna's head, expecting to be seen as soon as Krishna opened his eyes. Arjuna, sent by the Pandavas, reached soon after. His natural humility made him occupy a seat at Krishna's feet.

When Krishna opened his eyes, the first to be seen by him was Arjuna.

The situation was piquant. Since Duryodhana came first, he had a claim to Krishna's support. But since Arjuna was the first to be seen by Krishna, he too had a claim — perhaps a greater claim to his support. Krishna decided to help both. One was to get the services of his heroic army and the other was to get his personal guidance. Arjuna, being the younger of the two, was granted the privilege to choose. Arjuna preferred Krishna's personal help to the assistance of his great army.

Who does not know what happened in the Mahabharata war? Under Krishna's unerring guidance, the

Pandavas won a glorious victory over the Kauravas. Krishna then returned to Dwaraka and resumed ruling peacefully.

But a curse was cast on him.

Gandhari, the mother of the Kaurava brothers, firmly believed that if Krishna had so wished, the tragic war could have been avoided. At night, as she walked through the deserted battlefield with a lamp in her hand, surveying the faces of her dead sons, she was overwhelmed with agony and uttered a deadly curse. She said that Krishna's own people – the dynasty of the Yadavas – would be altogether destroyed within a few years, just as her children had been destroyed.

The time soon came for the curse to realise itself. One day, the unruly and unworthy youth of the great Yadavas teased a great sage. The sage cursed them once again.

A few days later, the Yadavas went on an excursion to the seashore at Prabhasa. There they got drunk and quarrelled among themselves. Soon the quarrel resulted in a wild free-for-all. No male member of the family, except Krishna, survived this suicidal fight.

Tired, Krishna was relaxing beneath a tree in a nearby forest. A hunter mistook his feet for the ears of a deer and shot an arrow. That ended the life of Krishna.

Upon hearing of this tragedy, Arjuna hurried to Dwaraka. Dwaraka lay under an eerie silence, broken only by the wailing of the Yadava women. Arjuna took charge of them on the way. Bandits attacked them and Arjuna could not defeat them because, with the passing away of Krishna, he had become powerless.

Once a paradise, Dwaraka was now almost a wasteland. If this was not enough, Dwaraka was soon engulfed by the sea. For seven days, it remained submerged. All that was associated with the memory of Krishna had been erased by the time the land re-emerged. Yet, the earth of Dwaraka is sacred enough, and pilgrims consider it good luck to be able to breathe its air where, once upon a time, Krishna ruled as king.

The temple at Dwaraka, which is dedicated to Krishna, stands on the banks of the river Gomati in a peaceful and serene atmosphere. It is said that one of the descendants of Krishna, Vajranath, built the temple.

Krishna has been worshipped at Dwaraka since time immemorial, though the original temple must have

been replaced several times in the distant past, with each new construction taking the place of the old. The four-handed, graceful image of Krishna looks vibrant with spirit.

It was in this temple that Mira, one of the supreme singers of Krishna's glory, passed the last years of her life. She had been the queen of a state in Rajasthan. But in her palace she was harassed by the members of her own family for her intense devotion to Krishna. She therefore, left the palace and came away to Dwaraka to meditate on Krishna in peace.

Later, her kinsmen repented and came to take her back. She refused to go. When they insisted, she entered the shrine of Krishna and shut herself in. When the doors of the shrine were forced open, Mira's sari was seen on the idol, but there was no trace of her. She is said to have physically merged with Krishna.

Refuge by the Bay ~ Mahavalipuram

THE SHRINES OF MAHAVALIPURAM

Pagodas with a difference

great king was once performing a *yajna* (calling upon supernatural powers through a fire ceremony) on the outskirts of his capital by the sea. Thousands of priests had come from all over the country to participate in the ceremony. The convener of the *yajna*, the king, had grown famous, not only throughout the earth, but also beyond it, in the regions of the heavens. Men were never tired of praising him, for he was extremely generous and kind; but the gods in heaven were afraid of him, for he defied them.

According to tradition, a king performing a *yajna*, was required to satisfy his guests, priests and Brahmins,

by granting them anything they wanted. This particular king, Vali or Mahavali, was extremely proud of his wealth and power. He had declared that there was nothing he could not grant when asked.

At sunset, when the king's alms-giving was ending for the day, a dwarf-like Brahmin appeared before him.

"What can I do for you?" asked the king.

"O mighty king! I want nothing but enough space to keep my feet comfortably," said the Brahmin.

Those around the king laughed at the little stranger's funny request. How much space would the Brahmin need to keep his tiny feet? Anyone could have given him what he wanted! It was a pity he had approached such a great king on such as auspicious day with such a poor request!

"Well, choose any place, on earth or in heaven, and place your feet as comfortably as you can! Upon my honour, the place is yours!" said the king with a benign smile.

No one could have imagined in his wildest dreams what the dwarf was going to do. For, the stranger's feet went on enlarging. Soon, the entire earth was barely sufficient to accommodate his one foot! He put his other

foot on heaven, and heaven was full with it ! To the amazement of the king, the Brahmin said, "My feet have covered both earth and heaven fully. Yet I have a third foot. Where can I keep it ?" As he said this, a third foot emerged from his navel.

Without a moment's hesitation, the king bowed down and pointed to his own head. The Brahmin placed his third foot on the king's head. The king went down — down till he reached *Patala*, the nether world. In a moment, a mighty and proud king, had been tamed by a dwarf.

The dwarf of course, was none other than the fifth incarnation of Vishnu — Vamana.

King Mahavali was the grandson of Prahlad, the illustrious devotee of Vishnu, whose non-believing father, Hiranya Kashyipu, had been killed by Narasimha, the fourth incarnation of Vishnu.

Mahavali too, was a true devotee of Vishnu. But he had one defect — pride — a vice which God always dislikes. It was out of his love for Mahavali that Vishnu came down to earth to teach humility to his proud devotee. It was also necessary to isolate Mahavali from earth and heaven.

Many people think the place Mahavalipuram was the city of King Mahavali in ancient times.

About 64 kilometres from Madras, Mahavalipuram, on the sea, is a charming place with its famous pagodas. These pagodas are carved in the form of *rathas*, or chariots, out of hillocks. All construction normally begins with the foundations. But these chariot-shaped temples were carved from their peaks downward, or from the surface inward.

Thus, out of rocks, these wonders of art and sculpture were born. The pagodas are dedicated to Yudhisthira, Bhima, Arjuna and Draupadi. The eleven-metre-high temple of Yudhishthira is the biggest of all.

These rock-cut monuments speak of a very advanced school of sculpture which developed in South India before the 6th century. Time destroyed all the achievements of this school, except those seen at Mahavalipuram, built under the patronage of the famous Pallava king, Narasimha Varman. The king's title was Mamalla; the place was known as Mamallapuram, after the regal title. The present name of the place owes its origin to this.

Narasimha Varman's son, Rajasimha Varman, is believed to have built the Shore Temple with the deities, Shiva and Vishnu, in it. High waves besiege this lonely and majestic temple making it a magnificent sight.

On a gigantic rock-face near the temple are carved some significant scenes from our epics, which appear elegant and lively even after so many centuries. The finest of these scenes is Arjuna's Penance; it covers an area of more than 300 metres and is one of the largest of its kind in the world.

A renowned son of India, C.V.Raman, writes: "Sitting on its gate-stone and gazing out at the never-ending turmoil of waters, one may meditate on India's great past and her present state. Dotting the country around, and defying the ravages of time, stand the magnificient monolithic temples and inimitable rock-carvings of Mahavalipuram. The dullest mind cannot fail to be stirred by the sight of such ancient architectural and artistic remains."

Gateway to God ~ Hardwar

Shrines Amid
the Citadel of Snow

Hardwar, Badrinath, Kedarnath

"Among mountains, I am the Himalaya," says Krishna in the *Gita*. Indeed, Himalaya, or the Citadel of Snow, is not only a sacred range of mountains to Indians, but also is the source of their life, and the soul of their culture. Rivers such as the Ganga, Jamuna, Saraswati, Brahmaputra and Sindhu, which enrich the Indian land and nurture the Indian people, are gifts of the Himalaya.

"At a height of about four-and-a-half kilometres slumber the sacred lakes, eternally mirroring in their still waters only the heavens and the mountain wilderness that cradles them," describes a Russian traveller, Zenaide Ragozin.

Supreme Place of Pilgrimage ~ Badrinath

Indian poets from Valmiki to Kalidasa, and from Kalidasa to Tagore, have derived great inspiration from the splendour of the Himalaya.

The Himalaya is also the abode of the Divine Mother. The Goddess Parvati is the daughter of the Himalaya. With her is identified one of the great peaks, the Gouri Shikhar. Her consort, Shiva, also dwells in the same mysterious and sacred region, and with him is identified Mount Kailas.

Many great sages had their hermitages there and the famous *tirthas,* the holy places of the Himalaya, have been the physical and spiritual destinations of innumerable people through the ages.

We have devoted a separate chapter to the cave temple of Amarnath. Let us now have a bird's-eye view of the temples of Hardwar, Kedarnath and Badrinath.

The Ganga, after meandering for over 800 kilometres through the labyrinth of the mountains, descends to the plains at Hardwar, which was for a long time known as Kapilasthan, because a great sage, Kapila, lived there in days gone by.

At Hardwar is situated the sacred *kund,* Hari-ki-Charan, or the Foot of Vishnu. It is considered a privilege

Threshold of Eternity ~ Kedarnath

to have a dip in its water. On its wall can be seen the footprint of Vishnu. Near Hari-ki-Charan there are several temples including the famous Gangadwara. Nearby there are many *ghats,* or sacred bathing spots. In the mountain walls which surround Hardwar there are many natural caves. These have provided shelter to devotees since time immemorial.

The ancient town of Hardwar bears the memory of many dramatic happenings. Kankhol, near Hardwar, was once the home of king Daksha, the father of Sati, an incarnation of Parvati.

Sati, one of the fifty daughters of Daksha, was married to Shiva. But for some vain reason, Daksha was very displeased with Shiva.

Once, Daksha decided to perform a rare rite known as the *Brihaspati Yajna.* For this occasion he invited many sages and kings, and all his daughters and their husbands, except Sati and Shiva!

But when Sati heard of the *yajna,* she arrived at her father's house, uninvited and unannounced. She knew that according to Indian tradition, a father's doors could never be shut to his daughter. Unfortunately, Daksha forgot this. At the very sight of Sati he burst into a tirade against Shiva.

His words fell harshly on Sati's ears. Her love and reverence for her husband were so deep that she could not bear the abuses. But what could she do or say to her father ? Out of anguish and despair she collapsed – she was no more.

Soon the tragic news reached Shiva. Trembling with fury, he pulled out a lock of his hair and dashed it to the ground. A spirit, Birabhadra by name, sprang up and mobilised an army of supernatural beings in no time.

Under Birabhadra's command, the unusual army soon reached Daksha's palace and destroyed everything. Daksha himself was beheaded and his head was consumed by the fire lit for the *yajna*. Later, when Shiva calmed down and agreed to restore life to Daksha, a goat's head was secured and fixed on his neck.

Shiva placed the dead body of Sati on his shoulders. Heart-broken, he roamed about here and there. A long time passed. At last, Vishnu, used his weapon, the Sudarsana Chakra, to cut the dead body into pieces. Wherever a fragment of Sati's body fell, there sprang a shrine and the place became holy.

There is a well at Kankhol – Satikund – believed to be the spot where Sati sacrificed her body. There are several sacred places around Hardwar associated with mythological events.

There is Kushavarta where Sage Dattatreya used to meditate. The river Ganga, while coming down from her secret abode in the upper regions of the Himalaya, playfully swept away the belongings of the sage. The sage's belongings, of course, were nothing more than a stick and jug. But the sage became so angry, that he was about to utter a terrible curse which would have brought an end to the flow of the Ganga. Fortunately, Brahma himself appeared before the sage and reminded him that, after all, it was a matter of great joy that the Ganga was flowing on to the earth! The sage was pacified only when Brahma promised to bless the place by his permanent presence.

At a distance of about 290 kilometres from Hardwar, at a height of more than 3000 metres, is situated the famous temple of Badrinath. It is surrounded by mountains which rise to a height of 7000 metres. On one side stands the grand Narayan Parvat, wrapped up in silver-hued snow; on the other side flows the Alakananda.

The deity, Badrinarayan, is a manifestation of Vishnu. The beautiful image is seen in a meditative mood with a variety of jewels covering his body. A canopy of gold is suspended over his head.

Though Badrinath is a very ancient holy place, the temple and the deity lay neglected and forgotten for a long time, thanks to the remoteness of the area. The temple was ruined and the deity somehow got immersed in the Alakananda. It was Shankaracharya who, through meditation, traced the deity. He restored the deity to its original seat, over which the temple was rebuilt.

For about six months in the year, the region remains covered with snow and, consequently, the temple remains closed. It is as though Nature had reserved the place exclusively for herself. During this period, a representative idol of Badrinarayan is worshipped at Joshimath. But before the doors of the temple are closed for the winter, the chief priest lights a lamp filled with ghee and puts it near the deity. The lamp remains lit till the day the temple is reopened six months later.

The same process is followed in the case of the temple of Kedarnath. The Pandava brothers, during their

last journey through the Himalaya camped for some time at Kedarnath. Draupadi was already dead before their arrival, and the youngest of the Pandavas, Sahadeva, breathed his last there.

Amid the enchanting beauty of the place, the Pandavas sat down and meditated to invoke the grace of Lord Shiva. Since then, Shiva has been worshipped at Kedarnath.

When the path to Kedarnath is blocked by snow, the representative deity of Kedarnath is worshipped at Ukhimath.

Seat of the Mother Goddess ~ Kalighat

Temple of the Mother Goddes

Kalighat in Calcutta

ɧundreds, of years ago, when there was no sign of the city of Calcutta, on the quiet bank of the Bhagirathi (another name for the Ganga), a poor Brahmin named Atma Ram used to sit and meditate every evening. Behind him was a dense forest. Darkness engulfed the area soon after sunset.

One evening, after his meditation, when Atma Ram stooped to wash his face in the river, he saw a luminous ray emanating from a certain point under the water. He remembered the spot and, early next morning, went there to have a closer look at it.

The water was as transparent as glass and in the light of the early dawn, the Brahmin could see a bright piece of stone lying on the river-bed. He picked it up and saw that it was shaped like a beautiful, graceful toe.

The toe-shaped stone could not be of much worth but, as Atma Ram held it in his hand, he felt great joy in his heart. He put it carefully in a safe place inside the forest and remained gazing at it for a long time, admiring it and feeling attracted towards it more and more.

Then, when after a day's wandering and work, Atma Ram went to bed, he dreamt a wonderful dream. He saw Sati, the consort of Shiva, dying of shock when her father, King Daksha, abused her husband; he saw the grief-stricken Shiva begin his aimless journey with the dead body of Sati on his shoulders; and finally, Vishnu cutting the dead body into pieces with his Sudarsana Chakra. Atma Ram also saw a toe of Sati fall into the Bhagirathi. He realised then that what he had picked up from the river-bed was the same toe, now transformed into stone.

Atma Ram probably erected a small hut in the forest and worshipped the toe there. In course of time, the devotee must have felt the urge to give a more concrete form to the goddess. However, we do not know for certain

when a full-fledged idol of Kali was installed there and when the first temple was built.

It is said that a pious landlord, Santosh Roy Chowdhury, who lived in the latter half of the 18th century, was sailing by the forest. It was evening. Suddenly, he heard someone blowing a conch-shell inside the forest. He saw the image of Kali being worshipped by a hermit. Roy Chowdhury was a person gifted with mystic insight and he instantly felt the presence of the Divine Mother in the image.

Soon he returned with men and money. He began to build a temple which was completed by his successors in the first half of the 19th century.

The deity became more and more widely known. As time went by, more and more people came to worship her and many settled down there. The forest gradually disappeared. The place became known as Kalighat. It was recognised as one of the foremost seats of the Mother Goddess.

Many people think that the name of the city of Calcutta was derived from the world Kalighat.

THE GRAND OLD SEAT
OF VISWESWAR

The Viswanath Temple of Varanasi

One of the holiest places for the Hindus is Kashi. It is also known as Varanasi because two lines of the Ganga, Varun and Asi, flow by it.

Along the banks of the river Ganga there are a number of beautiful ghats or bathing places, where people take holy dips.

The city has more than 1500 temples, including Buddhist shrines. The chief deity of the city is Visweswar, another name for Shiva. His abode is the famous Viswanath temple.

We do not know for certain who initiated the worship of Shiva at Varanasi. But during the reign of King

Dibodas, in the age of the Puranas, Visweswar once got disgusted with the king and retired to Mount Mandar. The god, of course, missed his home town, but he did not wish to return as long as Dibodas ruled the city.

Visweswar sent his spirit-servants to remove Dibodas. But they did not dare come face-to-face with the king and passed their time living near Manikarnika Ghat. Visweswar then sent the Sun God. He too failed to oust Dibodas. Many more came, but none returned. They were happy to stay on at Varanasi. Such was the charm of the city!

Visweswar had thought that after his departure the town would be reduced to misery. But it continued to be prosperous and happy. This was possible because King Dibodas was a man of great virtue. His good fortune, which was the result of his good deeds and sublime thoughts, was shared by his subjects.

After some time, Ganesha came to see Dibodas. He came in the guise of an astrologer. He impressed the king by his power to recall events that had occurred in the past and predict the events to come. The king was eager to attain salvation and enquired of the disguised god how

to realise it. Ganesha told him that a Brahmin would soon come down from the north and would give him the clue to attain salvation.

In the meantime, Visweswar sent Vishnu to King Dibodas. Vishnu came as a Brahmin, and since he came from the north, Dibodas asked him to show him the way to salvation. Vishnu told the king to seek the grace of Shiva. That inspired king Dibodas to build a new temple for Shiva. The self-exiled Shiva, pleased at last, returned to his old familiar city.

The temple of Visweswar is neither very high nor very big, but its crown is covered with gold. The present temple was built by Ahalyabai, the celebrated queen of Indore. Ranjit Singh, the Lion of Punjab, contributed the gold that covers the crown.

Varanasi has always been a must for Hindu pilgrims. To have a glimpse of Visweswar brings one great peace and serenity. To die at Kashi means attaining salvation.

Varanasi has been visited by great prophets and saints through the ages. Among them were Buddha, Shamkara, Ramanuja, Kabir, Nanak, Tulsidas and Sri Chaitanya Dev.

The Power of Shakti ~ Kamaksha

THE GODDESS OF FOLKLORE

The Temple of Kamaksha

Hundreds of Indian folktales tell us of the shrine of the goddess Kamaksha. According to these tales, it was not for an ordinary human being to approach the place where she dwelt. Only magicians and *tantriks*, riding enchanted flying trees, could go there at night. The region was frequented by ghosts and ghouls who naturally were weird in their conduct towards human beings. Only if a seeker was brave enough to risk an encounter with these fearful beings could he then enter the temple and worship the goddess. If the goddess was pleased, the seeker could gain mastery over many supernatural powers. He could perform miracles.

Even today, there are thousands of magicians in India who end their *mantras* with: "I command this to be done in the name of Goddess Kamaksha."

Though Kamaksha is popularly associated with *tantrik* beliefs, mystic experiences could come to people who were her sincere devotees.

The temple of Kamaksha is one of the main temples dedicated to the Mother Goddess in India. Mythology and folklore give us many stories about the origin of the temple. It is generally believed that it was built where a part of the dead body of Sati, the wife of Shiva, fell after Vishnu had cut it asunder with his Sudarsana Chakra.

We do not know who built the original temple of Kamaksha, but it was destroyed by the fanatic Kalapahar in the 16th century.

Soon afterwards, Malladeva, the Koc king of Assam, went on an expedition to conquer Bengal. In the battle that was fought between Malladeva and the Sultan of Bengal, Malladeva was badly beaten and his brother, Sukladeva, was captured by the Sultan.

At night, Sukladeva saw Kamaksha in his dream. She told him that it was wrong to fight a battle while the

temple of their goddess lay in ruins. Sukladeva realised their blunder. He was told by Kamaksha, as the dream continued, that he would be released when he cured the Sultan's mother who would soon be bitten by a snake.

In awhile, Sukladeva was called upon to try and cure the Sultan's mother as all other efforts had failed. Sukladeva, by the grace of Kamaksha, proved successful and was set free.

Sukladeva and Malladeva then devoted their attention to building a new temple over the ruins of the old one. It is said that the new temple was built with bricks baked in ghee.

Today it is easy to visit the shrine of Kamaksha which can be seen on the beautiful Nila hill in Assam, about four and-a-half kilometres from the city of Gauhati. Dozens of buses run every day from the city to the foot of the hill. From there, there are lighter vehicles for the temple.

Inside the temple there is a cave. Inside the cave stands a block of stone, symbolizing the deity. There is no image of the goddess. The mode of worship, too, is flexible. A visitor can worship according to the rites he is accustomed to.

A great number of people visit the temple during festivals like Durgapuja and Manasapuja.

To this day, Kamaksha remains the symbol of man's urge to achieve mastery over the secret laws of the occult world.

The Great Temple ~ Somanath

The Temple that Defies Destruction

The Temple of Somanath

The remains of the temple of Somanath "withstood the shocks of time and survived the attacks of destroyers. Aged, infirm, desecreated, it stood when Sardar Patel rescued it from neglect and pledged himself to its reconstruction. As a temple, it had done its work to remind ages of what India's faith had been; it was left only a symbol of her to-be-forgotten misfortune. With the dawn of a new era, the new temple has risen like the phoenix, from its own ashes," wrote K.M.Kunshi in 1950. His words gained new significance when, on 11 May 1951, Babu Rajendra

Prasad, then President of India, inaugurated a new shrine dedicated to Somanth.

K.M.Munshi writes: "The shrine of Somanath in Prabhasa is traditionally as old as creation; it is prehistoric." He further observes: "Prabhasa was traditionally a sacred place even in the days of Dharma, the son of Pandu. The *Mahabharata* refers to it again and again. It was very well-known to the people and was situated at a holy spot where the river Saraswati flowed into the sea."

Soma is the name for the moon, who was the son-in-law of Daksha. Once Soma disobeyed a certain instruction of his father-in-law. Daksha was so angry that he cursed him, saying, "thou shalt wane!"

The moon, who used to shine in full splendour every night till then, started to shrink. However, before the curse brought about an absolute end to the moon, many a god requested Daksha to revoke his curse. Daksha asked Soma to take a bath in the sea at the mouth of the river Saraswati and then to pray to Lord Shiva.

Thus Soma came to Prabhasa and worshipped Shiva. Hence at Prabhasa, Shiva came to be known as Somanath, the Lord of the moon. It is said that since then the moon comes to bathe in the sea at Prabhasa on every

Amavasya, or full dark night, after which he gradually recovers his lost splendour.

The first temple of Somanath was built as early as, if not earlier than, the 1st century A.D. Six hundred years later, when Dharasena IV ruled over a part of Gujarat, a new temple replaced the old one. But the second temple did not last long. We do not know whether it was attacked and destroyed by men, or if some natural calamity befell it or a defect in its construction caused its ruin. But the temple became more famous after it was built for the third time, in the ninth century.

Life around the temple was marked by peace and sanctity until on a January day in the year 1026, Mahmud of Ghazni struck. For three days, fierce resistance was offered by the people who least expected such a brutal assault on a temple. Fifty thousand men laid down their lives in a brave effort to save the deity, if not the monument, but Mahmud succeeded in plundering and destroying the shrine and he did not spare the deity either.

However, a new temple was built soon thereafter. That was replaced by a fifth and a more impressive one. This was built by the great scholar-devotee, Bhava Brihaspati, under the patronage of King Kumarapala, in the 12th century.

For a period of 100 years, the temple became a centre of religious and cultural research. Then Alla-ud-din Khilji sent his general, Alaf Khan, to destroy the grand monument Bhava Brihaspati had built with such devotion. This happened in the late 13th century.

The temple was reconstructed for the sixth time, by Mahipal, the king of Junagadh, and the deity was reinstalled by his son in the first half of the 14th century.

In the 15th century the temple was occupied, if not destroyed, by a young governor of Gujarat, Mahmud Begda, and the deity was exiled. But after a few years, Begda's hold slackened, and the deity was reinstalled.

In the beginning of the 18th century, there was yet another ghastly attack. Aurangzeb ordered Mohammad Azam to reduce the temple to dust. Azam did his job well! But the temple rose again under the patronage of the pious Queen of Indore, Ahalyabai, in the latter half of the 18th century.

The British, when they came to India, knew what a delicate place the shrine of Somanath occupied in Indian hearts, and how much the people had suffered because of all that had happened to the great temple.

One day in the year 1842, Edward Ellenborough, then Governor-General of India, made this exciting announcement:

"Our victorious army bears the gates of the temple of Somanath in triumph from Afghanistan, and the despoiled tomb of Sultan Mahomed looks upon the ruins of Ghazni.

"The insult of eight hundred years is at last avenged. The gates of the temple of Somanath, so long the memorial of your humiliation, are become the proudest record of your national glory, the proof of your superiority in arms over the nations beyond the Indus.

"To You, Princes and Chiefs of Sirhind, of Rajwarra, of Malwa, and of Guzerat, I shall commit this glorious trophy of successful war.

"You will yourselves, with all honour, transmit the gates of sandalwood through your respective territories to the restored temple of Somanath."

Michael Edwardes comments: "The farce lies not only in the supreme pomposity of the proclamation but in the fact that the gates were not from Somanath at all."

For one British Governor eager to create the impression that he could be a champion of the native cause,

there were many British bureaucrats who should be held responsible for the deterioration of the temple built by Queen Ahalyabai. The Gaekwad of Baroda, entrusted with the management of the temple, was for a long time denied the right to repair it.

However, soon after India achieved independence, in November 1947, Sardar Vallabhai Patel, the Deputy Prime Minister of India, visited the temple. It was the New Year Day of Samvat 2004. Addressing a mammoth gathering before the temple, he said: "On this auspicious day of the New Year, we have decided that Somanath should be reconstructed. You, people of Saurashtra, should do your best. This is a holy task in which all should participate."

Amidst the historic ruins, the new shrine of Somanath smiles today – a smile of undying faith.